LEGACY
HEIST

THE MISSING TREASURE IN AMERICA

Life-Story of Frank J. Williams

As Told By:
Lance Brazelton

For permission request, contact the following email
legacyheist@frankjwilliams.org

Written by: Lance Brazelton

Story Consultant: Julian Jay Burton

Edited by: Anita Cross, Doorress Anderson

Cover Design(Painting): John "Jahni" Moore

Graphic Design: Barbara Upshaw

Published by: Frank J. Williams (FJW Enterprises)

ISBN-13: 978-0-578-67723-1

Library of Congress Control Number has been applied for.

FRANK J WILLIAMS

Contents

Official Definition

Legacy Heist
noun
1.   A strategic plan designed to eradicate generational poverty.
"His legacy heist changed the dynamics of his family tree."

2.   A blueprint to generational wealth beyond money.
"Her great grandchildren will benefit from information documented in her legacy heist."

3.   A letter of truth written to the next generation of one's family.
"Their ancestor's legacy heist educated them on their current responsibilities."

4.   A universal movement that demands action in the barriers of your own home.
"If you fail to initiate your legacy heist; you will erase yourself from existence when you had the opportunity to erase the problem."

synonyms: master plan, blueprint, formula, recipe, roadmap
leg·a·cy heist

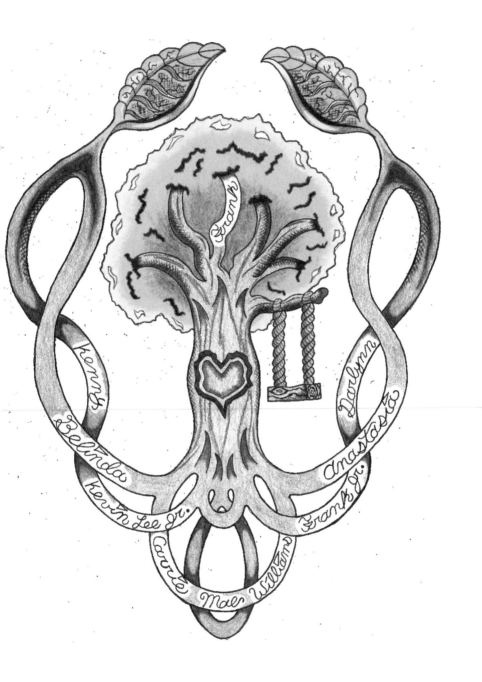

LEGACY

HEIST

Chapter 1

Poverty Pills

"If poverty was a prescription, the entire world would have this pill popping addiction."

Poverty is a pill the world has chosen to swallow on a daily basis. This mental drug has been abused since slavery, and a large percentage of the world is incarcerated in a conundrum called generational poverty.

You're an animal without a stimulus if you look at poverty affected neighborhoods with a zoo-like mentality. If you believe you can cover up all your problems with a blanket of money, then it's not a coincidence that you've never been happy. Poverty isn't merely the state of being extremely poor physically, but it's also the state of being extremely poor mentally.

Life can be a dream. Have you ever wondered why some celebrities, athletes, and entertainers end up broke like they were literally not living their dream? It's because poverty was a pest on their property, and they lacked the pesticide called legacy.

It's possible for a talented, or skilled individual to become successful so quickly, that they never take the time to plant legacy into their life; during the fertilization phase of their career. When you're dirt poor you're in the fertilization phase. The principles you plant in this beginning stage play a major role in the harvest you'll eventually grow. Therefore, you need to know how to manage a million dollars before it even touches your hands. Learn legacy so you can provide a stepping stool for generations after you; and understand that poverty has always been the resource that provided fuel, when you were speeding down the roads to riches. America will tell you that money makes the world go 'round, but you can't possess it without work. We have jobs so we can attempt to run away from poverty. You can be financially free, but how do you escape the prison called poverty when you're incarcerated mentally?

If you neglect this question, your life's work can become a life sentence. You'll be erased from history like an inmate erased from society; eternally trapped in a system that's not designed for you to ever break free. Your family tree will become dehydrated generations into the future, because when you had all the money in the world you forgot to plant the one seed that would feed them for eternity...legacy.

Regardless of how deep your pockets may be, you've failed if your legacy doesn't have roots that are just as deep! I pray this quote sparks controversy and gets the attention it needs. Let me show you how to share the dinner table with your great grandkids' generations into the future.

Some of the wealthiest people in the world don't feel complete when they look at their reflection; because, they still see a missing puzzle piece. They don't know where to find it. However, it's so valuable it's literally free, and it was never lost if you look into the life-story of this kid from Milwaukee.

It was 1965 and the civil rights movement was on the brink of changing the course of American history. Many lost their lives during this pivotal time in history, but their sacrifices were not in vain. It was the breakdown that gave America the breakthrough to becoming the greatest country in the world for opportunity. The gates of equality were unlocked for all Americans.

In the midst of these historical moments, these events became more memorable for women bringing new lives into the world; because their children would be exposed to a variation of America that granted equality to every citizen. One of these special ladies was Carrie Williams who lived in Duncan, Mississippi.

Mother Carrie didn't participate in the Civil Rights Movement taking place in the South, because she didn't like the negative effects on the environment around her.

So instead of marching south to Selma, Mother Carrie marched north to Joliet, Illinois, and later found a home in Milwaukee, Wisconsin.

She went north in an attempt to create a better environment for the child she had cried and prayed for. Although her child's father wasn't marching alongside her, she was still thankful that she was blessed to have a child.

Her baby boy took his first breath in this evolving world of opportunity.

On May 8, 1965… Frank J. Williams was born.

Who is your Mother Carrie?

Hint:

You wish they could live forever.

Chapter 2

Legacy in Cursive

"Legacies are lost, and dreams are disoriented at night; because we've allowed society to write the narrative of our life."

The majority of families living in poverty don't know their origins. You'll feel like a ghost; because, you're cursed with an erased past and haunted by the uncertainty of your future.

Family origins are the roots of the family tree. When an individual doesn't know their family history, they tend to branch out in the wrong direction. They follow the wrong voices, join the wrong crowds; educate themselves with false information, and live on faulty principles. Ironically, those same people can't figure out why they're not happy with where they are in life.

During the late 1960s and 70s, America was trying to heal itself from the wounds of the Civil Rights Movement. It left a scar on America which we were supposed to view as a reminder. However, America had problems trusting the healing process of this change, and tended to peel off the scab before it could heal. America stared at its own imperfections so hard, that the nation forgot to notice how beautiful its reflection was becoming.

America was on the verge of becoming a more mature nation; but, a series of immature acts left us paused in the past. You can't expect a flower to blossom if you cut off the bud every time it starts to sprout. Many lives were lost during this healing process including Martin Luther King Jr. who watered his dream until it grew into existence.

America had lowered the drawbridge to equality and we were free at last!

But one question was never answered…

Where do we go from here?

If you fast forward a few years, you'll notice during the early 1970s gangs emerged from the shadows and became territorial. There was an increase in the poverty rate and people started killing their own race. People started fighting each other since they no longer knew what to fight for.

The same demographic that once came together peacefully protesting for equality, started marching backwards. It was like they unlocked the gate gaining access to what they yearned for; but forgot how to collaborate with each other once arriving on the other side.

We've allowed society to write a bad narrative about us. We've been stuck on the same page like a bookmark, because no one comprehended where we should've gone from there. The leaders and influential figures of that era didn't have the answers because,

"where we should've gone from there" was not their assignment.

We'll never forget the powerful images of the Civil Rights Movement because everyone who played a role has a coffin resting on our conscience. We celebrate their life's work through memorials, monuments, museums, historical months, and reserved holidays. However, no one wants to admit that we've failed them. We did not fail them as a race, community, region, or state. We failed they as a nation because Lady Liberty doesn't know how beautiful she really is. She hides behind a false color and we paint a portrait of her that doesn't reveal the truth behind her scars.

We shouldn't be ashamed to talk about these scars because they remind us of our nation's truth. The truth tells us exactly how far we've come and highlights the areas where we can still improve!

In today's society, we sometimes forget our progress, and treat each other like our history has deleted scenes. The educational system teaches us that America's history is merely a photo album.

The present generations view these images from the perspective of,

"How is this relevant to us?"

The youngsters exploring the interests that gravitated them toward these topics are interrogated by the older generations quoting,

"You weren't living during those time periods, so what do you really know about how it felt?"

If this is your attitude, you need to restart your brain the next time you go to sleep so you wake up with the realities of how America has evolved. Once your update is installed, don't pop quiz the next generation asking,

"what's wrong with them?"

When the information of where you went wrong was never on the chalkboard.

Now, we live in a nation where people tend to forget that it was the ugly moments in history that granted us access to see how beautiful the country is today.

America has never seen its reflection in 20/20 vision. The curse of not sharing our origins trickles down into each and every American family hiding the truth from their children. Don't be afraid of the pandora box on the shelf decorated in decades-old spider webs.

Millions of people are clueless of their purpose. It has brought them to a dead-end mentally and financially. Now they're merely making enough money to keep their noses above water. They don't know where to go from here; they've grown so far in the wrong direction; they've paved a route even further from their purpose in life.

Legacy is the sole purpose in life.

The next generation is supposed to be an upgrade of the previous generation, but this cannot be achieved if the ancestors of that family tree failed to plant a legacy. When the next generation steps up to the plate in this game called life; they should be able to stand on their ancestors' life work, and see further than they could ever see. Even if the next generation doesn't follow their ancestors' footsteps; they should at least be able to follow their principles. Therefore, the legacy of that family tree continues to grow regardless of the occupation chosen by the next generation.

The childhood trauma that Frank Williams experienced resonated from this same atmosphere. His ancestors planted a seed that grew a family tree, but they didn't plant a legacy to grow along with it. During the early stages of Frank's life in the 70's, he realized that his life lacked family origins and father figures who led by example. He would see glimpses of different men coming into his mother's life, but none of the relationships endured to the point of him understanding a father's role. He had an open wound on his heart that only his father could patch. It rooted so deep that he didn't even feel the pain of his absence. Frank became immune to his unfortunate upbringing. His father chose to be absent in his life nurturing children he had with other women. Since his biological father was never in his life, Frank didn't have any knowledge of what a father figure was or the benefits of having one present during the early stages of life. At that particular time, he didn't understand that his mother couldn't teach him everything. There were lessons best translated with a father figure in the household.

Never meeting his grandparents and an absent father promoted generational poverty in the images Frank saw on a daily basis.

Without a legacy growing at the same rate of your family tree; your family becomes brittle and breaks away from each other. Then the next generation lives with a reincarnated cursed that was merely dormant during their childhood years. If the next generation cannot benefit from the previous, it's almost like their ancestors never existed. This is how poverty is passed down the family tree like an heirloom.

Frank never accepted this family heirloom. He didn't know this at the time, but a dream he had at a young age gave him a glimpse of what his legacy had the potential to become. During the early stages of his life, Frank dreamed that one day he would write his name in cursive. He made this dream a concrete reality by writing his name religiously every single day.

He never had a father, grandparents, or any idea about his family origins; but for some odd reason, writing his name meant everything to him. It was as if he was proud to be part of a family tree he never knew. Frank wrote his name over and over on multiple sheets of paper at school. He wrote his name at home during all hours of the night. Frank adopted the habit of writing his name in this fashion from elementary school throughout his high school years.

Frank Williams in cursive meant the world to him but he could never figure out why.

Writing his name in cursive spoke volumes into his life because he finally started to get an identity of who he was. He didn't know his ancestors nor his own origins and at the same time was uncertain about his future. One thing that was crystal clear to him as a child is that his name had the opportunity to mean something, because he literally wrote it into existence.

Chapter 3

The Invisible War

"If poverty was a color it would be transparent; and if you're transparent along with it you'll see the root of the problem."

When you look closely at the demographics affected by different variations of poverty, you'll notice that they are feeding a trend that should have died a long time ago. In today's society, the only time this demographic comes together again is when a subject matter is broadcasted as,

'White America vs Black America.'

There is a thin line between hearing and listening. In order to understand why generational poverty is rooted so deeply, we must go back to the day Martin Luther King Jr. gave us his famous dream speech. America was so focused on the image of a black man addressing racial issues on a national stage, that we failed to listen to the heartbeat of what the message meant. His speech was received as the falling action of the Civil Rights Movement; but was also a battle cry simultaneously. He attempted to give us a glimpse of how inspirational the narrative of our nation could be. Remember, he called it a dream for a reason.

The underlining themes of our country is love, hope, opportunity, sacrifice, and positive change. These characteristics existed in the old testament of America's history, but no one wrote them into existence in the new testament of today's society.

While Nelson Mandela was incarcerated physically, the rest of the world was incarcerated mentally.

Boundaries, shackles, and chains were finally broken but America remained incarcerated mentally even when he said we were free at last. A trend of legacy would be rooted deep in the soil of our country if America wasn't behind bars mentally. We would have continued marching toward the doors of opportunity scattered across America; but because we didn't escape the penitentiary of our own minds we subliminally went backwards. We are blinded by a spotlight that glorifies how our nation is evolving, but behind that light lives the darkest truth about today's society... we haven't fully evolved along with it.

It's self-inflicted suicide; these incidents aren't limited to this demographic because it's no longer about race. Don't neglect what's in the shadows of America's face.

Both ethnicities are guilty of not investigating the strays from their own shade. The truth is no one is better than anyone else. We share the same responsibilities amongst the multiple opportunities our country has to offer. We're all Americans who live in the greatest country in the world. All we have to do is simply accept the positive change that already occurred. America as a whole doesn't know how to deal with itself because it has become so successful and complex.

Yes, some aspects of society are still corrupt; however, don't ignore the fact that the elephant in the room is the size of baby Dumbo and not his mama Mrs. Jumbo.

There is nothing wrong with protesting and picketing for the right cause. However, until you protest to your household about the broken branches in your family tree, you will continue to pass on the same generational curses that haunted you as a child, and followed you like the Grim Reaper for the rest of your life. The battle is not this race vs that race, rich vs poor, him against her, or you against me. The war that is taking place every single day is your legacy vs generational poverty, and the battlefield is your home where you lie your head every night. For generations your worst enemy has been hiding in plain sight because poverty was promoted in the images you've seen.

Regardless of your unfortunate upbringing, you can still win the fight for your family in the war against generational poverty.

Millions of children grow up in single parent households across America. Ignorance is truly bliss; because children are seeing but they do not pay attention to what's being given to their parents or how their parents navigate through life.

There's an invisible war taking place. Your children's minds are being ambushed by the images you may not realize you're promoting. Generational poverty is rooted so deep that families naturally feel their poverty driven home is a safe haven, when it's been the war zone of the real fight for generations.

Frank became aware at a young age of a common trend in his household; Mother Carrie always needed assistance to provide for him on a daily basis. Once he started observing the cycle of how his family operated, it sparked an interest in his young mind. He started yearning for the truth about his circumstances and family structure. Frank saw that his mother consistently needed food stamps and sometimes visited food banks available to the public.

They lived in the projects in Milwaukee, and Frank could never formulate the answers to why his family was so heavily dependent on government assistance. When he headed to school every day, he always saw a visual difference between his family and other people around the city.

Chapter 4

Christmas Gifts

"Christmas always seemed empty, because
the greatest gift Mother ever gave me
couldn't fit under the tree."

Frank didn't understand why Mother Carrie needed government assistance to keep food in his little tummy. He would always try to pinpoint the difference between his family and everyone else living in their neighborhood.

Children are free in their minds until they become convicted by the responsibilities of growing up. All a child may focus on is food, fun, what they like to do, and what their parents direct them to do until they get to this point. Happiness is a child's first priority; and keeping their light as bright as possible can sometimes blind them when looking at their parents. Children have so many expectations when they look at their parents. They can predict their every move based on what they've seen on a daily basis.

Children are like baby birds. When mother leaves the nest, it's embedded in the child's mind that she's automatically going to come back and have food for them when she returns. It's equivalent to going to work in order to provide.

Children focus on receiving but never question the hardships a parent may endure to keep a roof over their head. No good parent wants their child to see the struggles they deal with behind closed doors because they don't want to contaminate their child's young mind. When something in a parent's heart becomes troubled, they tend to keep it concealed so their child doesn't witness a glimpse of uncertainty. However, if a child starts to question their surroundings and challenge their circumstances, do not be afraid to reveal the truth unto them. The simple fact that they understand something is wrong at a young age, is concrete proof that they are the chosen ones in their family who will one day erase the poverty their family was drawing for generations.

Frank accepted his role at a young age. He questioned his circumstances and tried to bridge the gap in his mind between what made his family so different from everyone else.

When the holiday season rolled around, he saw the differences in his family through the decorations designed to get him into the Christmas spirit. Frank noticed that his home was one of the few houses in the neighborhood that didn't embody the Christmas spirit, physically.

Christmas wasn't the way Mother Carrie necessarily wanted it, but she did her best with what she could provide. She couldn't buy the toys she wanted Frank to have but she explained to him that one day he would grow up and have more than mama could ever give him.

Frank's mind had no concept of the world of Christmas on an average child's level. He was never able to walk into the world's promises and this helped clear the path to his purpose.

The decorations never became a distraction. You create a false narrative in your household when you spend everything you have, and your children know you don't have it to spare.

We're rushing to tell our children a lie! Now, our children think there's substance in their lives built with a pile of materialistic things.

If you spend every dead president in your pocket on Christmas gifts, not only will your wallet be empty... you will be empty, and your children will be empty as well. They just aren't saying it because they're too naive to know how empty materialistic things actually are.

People go nuts every holiday season; but when you pile gifts under the Christmas tree, generational gifts are being stolen from your legacy tree!

When your children are generationally fulfilled, Christmas gifts become empty boxes.

The real excitement is born when you have something they can look forward to. This is a gift that every generation has the opportunity to unwrap. Now your empty feeling doesn't exist.

The honest truth about unwrapping a Christmas gift is that when you tear the wrapping paper you become overwhelmed with a wave of emptiness. The shift in reality that causes this wave of emptiness is due to the fact that there was no truth in life transitioned from those physical gifts.

Mother Carrie's home wasn't glowing in Christmas lights like a bright star in the distance, and an inflatable Santa Claus wasn't smiling in the front yard. However, Frank did find a small Christmas tree once he entered his home. Although they couldn't celebrate Christmas the traditional way, it never stopped Mother Carrie from having a servant mentality because the gift of giving was her forte.

Although they didn't have much to spare, Mother Carrie was selfless and still blessed others in need with every opportunity she stumbled across.

Her servitude came into play after Frank was born. She wanted to do her best in her ability to keep him safe; and didn't want anything she did to fall back on him when it originally wasn't his problem. Although Santa Clause never visited their home, their house already had an angel who understood, and loved the wonderful gift of giving.

From a child's perspective, it frustrated Frank to see his mother freely giving away the little they did obtain. Little did he know that his frustration was a blessing in disguise. Mother Carrie's servitude was the biggest Christmas gift he could've possibly been given. He accepted it at an early age but didn't unwrap it until later in life.

Chapter 5

From Fear to Fruit

"Fear is the most fertilized soil, but whose assignment is it to nurture your vulnerabilities?"

Fear is like a barrier that stands between you and your purpose in life. Fear can make the stepping-stones to get to your purpose disappear before your eyes, even when you have a clear view of your purpose. Fear is equipped with vulnerability because you've never allowed yourself to gain strength in that specific aspect of your life. There's a secret that the world never told you... fear cannot survive in the outside world, only in your mind. When you take something out of its natural habitat, it's no longer able to survive based on the necessities of its existence. Fear can only survive in the mind because it acts like a lens when you look toward doing things differently. The fear that stands between you and your purpose might seem like the tallest hurdle ever; but remember, it only exists in your mind. You'll soon realize the hurdles that seem taller than the sky are merely illusions. Fear fades away when you gain the momentum to challenge your circumstances.

When Frank was seven years old, Mother Carrie was in an abusive relationship. One night his mother's abusive boyfriend was livid because she refused to open the door due to the abusive behavior he demonstrated before Frank's young eyes. Mother Carrie boiled a pot of hot water in desperation to keep him safe, and Frank closely observed the situation. All he knew was that he loved his mother more than anything in the world. It immediately took him out of his element to see her take extra precaution in an attempt to keep him safe. As the water came to a boil on the stove eye, tears shimmered in the eyes of her baby boy. Mother Carrie didn't want him to witness the possibility of what might happen. She also knew it would haunt him if she kept the truth of this moment locked away since he had already gotten a glimpse. The abusive individual had beaten on the door to the point that the door broke, and he forced himself into their home. His mother defended them to the best of her ability and even in the midst of drastic measures, Frank never left his mother's side. The consequences of his curiosity left scars from splashes of the boiling hot water.

Frank realized at a young age that everything in his life wasn't perfect, and this was the night when he really challenged the thought of,

"What's going on with my family, and what makes us so different?"

Although he didn't know what role to play in his family tree, he understood that sacrifices were going to have to be made in order to propel them forward. With no one else around to look up to, he turned to the mirror in search of the individual who would one day make those sacrifices. That's why the uncertainty of his future scared him the most.

An atmosphere of fear started following his family like a shadow; but he soon realized that even in the darkest moments the scariest clouds have a silver tint hidden inside them.

Even fear itself has vulnerabilities and if you target it every time you see it, you'll unlock the powers of your potential that you didn't know existed inside yourself. Fear is the most fertilized soil and there are benefits to planting seeds in this garden. If a child understands this at a young age, you'll hear them question their circumstances more than usual. This isn't something to get upset about. It's something you should embrace because it's an early sign of strength showing a child is strong enough to challenge their circumstances.

What was once fear to Frank became fruit he fed himself from. Fear was the seed that stimulated his maturity in not only challenging his circumstances but also yearning for a better life.

Mother Carrie made the sacrifice to stay at home on welfare because this was the only way she was able to keep security in her household. Her security when it came to family became a force field that couldn't be penetrated without her permission ever since she had to defend her baby from a toxic individual. Influences from the outside world could no longer contaminate the pureness that Frank kept in his heart; his safe haven was under his mother's roof. However, he would soon have to walk out the front door where his mother's security didn't exist. His mother could protect him but only when he was under her roof. When you have a pure heart, the outside world gravitates to you like a shark smelling blood.

The outside world tries to throw every negative label known to man at your profile picture. The world attaches negative labels to adolescents who make mistakes while ignoring the fact that these children lack guidance; ensuring they'll automatically have trouble in some aspects of life every time they walk out the front door of their single parent's security. Disoriented boys are stuck in the wrong narrative and disoriented girls are taken advantage of. Fatherless females yearn to have relationships with males because they are seeking security, structure, and protection. Far too often they end up with their hearts broken and taken advantage of due to gravitating towards the wrong images of what they think a real man looks like.

When a young child walks out the door every day; people don't have the magnitude to understand what must happen to ensure they make it back safely, develop in the right direction, not be guided by the wrong influences based on images their generation is attracted to, and how to trust in a world with lies lingering in the atmosphere.

Although it wouldn't have been intentional, at any given point in Frank's childhood he could have steered off course onto a direful destiny. Just one touch of direction and unconditional love could have changed his childhood. No one was there to provide it outside of his mother's security where he needed it the most.

Lack of family structure is always going to be part of society, but you navigate through it by seeking who's assigned to you at different stages of your life. When you are yearning and seeking the individuals assigned to you, you're better suited to attract what's meant for you instead of letting people pray upon you.

Chapter 6

One Meal a Day

"The man of the house is supposed to bring food home. So, will a child starve if they have no father to call their own?"

The man of the house has always been seen as the hunter and has the responsibility of bringing food home for his family. However, when there is no father figure in the household to play this role, the children under that roof become haunted by hungry thoughts. The excitement of their childhood is interrupted by growls of hunger in their stomachs. Their minds gravitate towards surviving on a daily basis instead of enjoying the beauty of being a kid.

When a father figure doesn't exist in a child's world, they turn to their single mothers and expect them to have all the answers to their hunger. In a dysfunctional home, hunger isn't defined as merely a weakness from lack of food. Children growing up in poverty are also starving for the truths behind their family and wish to be blessed with the wisdom of understanding. With the head of the household absent from his role, there's only one person left standing who the children turn to for answers...

their single mother. Single mothers are always in the line of fire when it comes to playing both roles of guardianship. Single parents are faced with many battles on a daily basis. When they're searching for the next meal to place on the table, their children are searching for ways to help them in return and most approach it the wrong way. Some adolescents resort to illegal activities solely based on the imagery making money in their environments. These teens are planting the right seeds; however, they are watering them with the wrong substance. If someone doesn't offer a helping hand to show them the different routes available to prosperity, their plan becomes a mistake in the making.

At eight years old, it was clear to Frank that although he didn't have a father present, he knew there was something he could do about being fatherless. Also, he welcomed two younger sisters into his world at this time, Darlynn and Belinda.

Frank was the only boy in a household full of women, and the concept of being the man of the house was constantly weighing on his shoulders. He was haunted by misunderstandings of what real men looked like. The only lead he had was the influence on emotions through his mother and two sisters.

Mother Carrie did everything she could to protect her children, but her umbrella of protection had a radius that only covered the square footage of her home. His mother could give him insight on emotions he felt while at home, but his scariest thoughts arose from emotions outside his home in the process of trying to upgrade to manhood. He continued to challenge his hungry thoughts on the environment they lived in. He soon realized it wasn't his environment that needed to be challenged; the target was his family's way of operation.

The world would have taught him that Mother Carrie did something wrong to keep him in bondage. People tend to play dodge ball with blame, but by simply opening a door of opportunity she opened the gate to who her baby boy really was.

Mother Carrie made the best out of the resources in her reach. An outsider never would have eaten some of her meals based on the appearance. Frank and his sisters were so thankful for the little they had that it felt like they were eating the most expensive caviar in the world.

Mother Carrie could only provide one warm meal a day. This bothered Frank to the point that he started to starve for not only change in his family's structure but also how to live instead of merely surviving. He was thankful for his mother's daily contributions, but he knew deep down inside that she was tired of driving the survival of a household by her lonesome. He made it his unspoken obligation that he would help her put food on the table for their family. This was the defining moment when he accepted his role as the man of the house. Although he was stepping into a pair of shoes that were way too big for a kid, he walked out his front door in search of a job since he finally found a purpose.

Who is your Belinda?

Hint:

They've been your road dog since the beginning, your guardian angel for eternity, and the gatekeeper to eliminate the enemies your tunnel vision could not see.

Chapter 7

Help Wanted

"I was merely a kid, but I accepted my role; and became a business owner at only eight years old."

Frank looked beyond his front porch in search of a job. While walking on his journey, he had flashbacks of when he and his mother would walk for miles to stand in line at food banks. The memories of Mother Carrie having to physically walk to simply feed him fueled his drive to continue marching. He knew his mother was in need of help and his sisters were in need of someone to look up to.

When a child simply yearns to make a difference for their family, they are preparing to initiate what it takes to complete the mission. Yearning is a side effect of finding a purpose, and acting upon it comes with acceptance.

When you finally find a purpose, the obstacles along the trail to achieve it can seem frightening almost like mission impossible. You'll stumble across a purpose when you yearn to make a difference for your family, but that purpose cannot be brought to reality without acceptance. Knowing your role and accepting your role are two totally different things. One cannot exist without the other. You'll get glimpses of what you have the potential to do but until you fully accept that role those visions will remain on the outskirts of reality. When you get a clear perspective of your role, sometimes it can be so overwhelming that you start to second guess yourself. This doesn't mean you lack the skills and ability to play the part; it's simply a side effect from growing up in an environment where poverty existed either physically or mentally in your family. Finding a purpose for yourself is like finding the key to a treasure chest. The poverty driven atmosphere around you sometimes alter your thoughts and makes you think you're not the chosen one; but nothing in this world is a coincidence!

Poverty forces you to experience life without elements that are essential to your growth. This lack has the power to create scotomas where you could've gotten access to better perspectives on life. Poverty places an invisible cloak on the blessings scattered around your environment, but when you finally accept your role everything you have the potential to change will be unveiled before your eyes.

Frank spotted his first blessing when he noticed a help wanted sign in the window of a local grocery store. He walked in with his confidence on his sleeve and humbly asked the first person he saw about the help wanted sign in the window. The individual he spoke with was a man named Mr. George who was the owner and operator of the grocery store.

Mr. George asked,

"Isn't it a little early for you to be looking for a job, son?"

The young Frank Williams responded by sharing his circumstances and his mission to help his mother put food on the table for their family.

Mr. George interviewed Frank on the spot, and realized that he was interviewing a young business owner like himself. Frank had three characteristics that glaringly stuck out to Mr. George... transparency, credibility, and integrity.

The transparency in Frank's reason for finding a job allowed Mr. George to see the world from his perspective. Through the windows of his eyes were images of his mother with a smile on her face. He knew if he got the job then she would finally get to take a breather for once. Mr. George saw himself through the transparency of Frank's character; an ambitious individual on the hunt to bring food home for his family. Mr. George was impressed to see a young individual yearning to make a difference and taking the road less traveled along the way. Mr. George knew if he answered his battle cry, he would not only be helping Frank; but he would also be lending a helping hand to a generation he wouldn't live long enough to see. Through the transparency of Frank's character, generations of ambitious individuals will grow from the seed Mr. George planted that day.

Mr. George gave young Frank a job at his grocery store. He would sweep and bag groceries while on the clock. Mr. George didn't just give him a job but an opportunity to change the images he had been seeing throughout his childhood. He could have easily gravitated towards the wrong narrative in the streets if he continued his search.

When disoriented children run away from home, they are eventually kidnapped by the uncertainty of their own lives. At eight years old, Frank ran away from home every single day; but he ran away so he could bring something back. Regardless of how much he loved his family; he understood that in order to make a difference for his family, he had to gain the courage to lose sight of them.

The action of bringing food back home was the sharpest purpose Frank saw for his life as a child, and it started to carve his character into existence.

Although Frank was her older brother, Belinda saw him as the father figure she never had. He was the only male she could look up to and he protected her from the ills of the world. He taught her at an early age that if she wants something in life, she's not entitled to it and she would have to work extremely hard for it.

When Belinda saw her brother bring food home, she accepted an identification of what a man is supposed to do for his family. So, she planned to look for that type of man in the future.

Frank didn't go straight home after school. When school ended in the evening, he went to work and came home later at night.

Mr. George had given Frank a new breath of life. He was feeding his mind with a purpose when Frank once couldn't identify his circumstances.

This was the moment he realized his family lacked the road map to their legacy. Frank made it his responsibility to initiate the war against his personal poverty to one day change the dynamics of his family tree.

This assignment came early but he was too young to identify the longevity of initiating this fight. He didn't identify it in the flesh or spirit, only in the physical world. However, all three identifications must be in sync in order to survive this war.

Do you have more than one Mr. George?

Hint:

They gave your children an opportunity, too; because they reached out a helping hand through you.

Chapter 8

Footsteps of Faith

"In the footsteps of faith, I had to step out; like a baby bird in Mama's nest I had to jump out."

Adolescents are misguided in today's world because they have followed a path that led them into trust issues. When Frank was fourteen years old, he became scared and double minded simply because he didn't know which voices to listen to.

Life becomes an arena when you grow up with trust issues. While locked inside this fight to the death you're mentally battling how to approach life. You have the way you grew up, the way you learned, the way people and images have influenced you, and the uncharted territory where your spirit says there's got to be another way. Yet, the same question is raised at every fork in the road,

"What if you go against everything you know?"

This uncertainty was the root of Frank's fear; however, this fear fades away when you figure out which voice to listen to.

You must mute the voices until you first create an identification within yourself. Just like the runway at the airport, it'll highlight the correct route for your life. You can unmute the voices echoing in the world once you've established this identity within yourself. Soon the right voice to listen to is going to gain more volume than the others and it'll speak to the identity you planted inside yourself. This equips your journey through life with a combination lock for security. You'll channel out all the wrong voices like it's second nature. It is essential that you stay true to what's secure to you, the voices that are eligible to speak to you, and the roadmap you believe in.

Now it boils down to this. What price are you willing to pay in order to stay the course; not only for your physical self, but for the identity you've created inside...your spiritual self.

It was Frank's experiences from being hypocritical, scared, and double minded that pinpointed out who he could and couldn't trust. In the midst of dodging all the wrong voices, there was one voice that never steered him the wrong way – the voice of Mother Carrie.

As an adolescent, Frank was upset because his mother was single and couldn't grant him everything he saw amongst his peers. However, he always trusted her. His father was never active in his life and he never came in contact with the ghosts of his grandparents' origins. He trusted his mother because she was all he knew. She was the familiar voice in his head at every fork in the road and her voice coached his conscience when identifying right from wrong outside of their home. His mother kept an umbrella of security over her home, but she always feared that her children lacked protection as they walked into the world on a daily basis. Her solution to keeping them within arms reach of her protection regardless of how far from home they may be, was to feed their inner spirit by encouraging them to get baptized. Mother Carrie's security was his motivation, but he personally wanted to get baptized because he was yearning for guidance from a higher power.

When he stepped into the water, he felt like a baby bird that had jumped from its mother's nest. Mother Carrie no longer worried because Frank was about to get his wings of security that would fly him to greater heights.

When he was submerged under water for the first time, a layer of protection wrapped around his life serving as an unbreakable shield.

He never feared making the wrong decisions, and never feared that the right decisions weren't available. Mother Carrie gave him access to faith before he could identify what faith really was.

Frank was already physically going out yearning for access; but this was the moment he started to grow and embody the spirit to fight this war internally. One of his greatest characteristics as a child is that he was always yearning for wisdom and knowledge in everything he saw.

When you walk by Faith it's peculiar to people. You're playing a role in something that's so much bigger than yourself. If you had known earlier, you would've gotten overwhelmed.

When you're the only one who sees the complete picture while everyone else merely sees a few pieces, you must walk by Faith and not sight. This is the only way to guide them into a world that they didn't know existed.

Chapter 9

Worst of both Worlds

"The mischief that I witnessed wasn't meant to be seen, take me to another world like a green screen."

Frank spent a lot of time at his friends' homes in the suburbs. They would invite him over for dinner and he always went since food was limited at home.

The first time he was extended an invitation he felt like he was being invited to a royal dinner. From the outside looking in, the suburbia kids lived in a perfect home. They had nice sized houses equipped with both parents and their bedrooms were filled with everything they could've possibly wanted, like they had a magic genie to grant their every wish.

However, since generational poverty was so deeply rooted in him, Frank started to get a glimpse of what life looked like when placed on a silver platter.

He got a sneak peak behind the scenes noticing that his peers kept secrets hidden from their parents.

Behind closed doors, his peers in the suburbs were more heavily involved in drugs and alcohol because their parents were rarely home. It caught him off guard because drug abuse was something that didn't exist in his own home due to the safety net of his mother's security. Frank never allowed his peers to pull him into their illicit drug use. He didn't partake because his passion for providing for his family kept him distracted; and disconnected him from the flame his friends were attracted to. He didn't try it even when temptation was on the tip of his tongue because he knew he wasn't strong enough to do it without it becoming suicidal. He didn't want to pacify the reality that he had learned to deal with so well. It would have weakened his spirit causing him to feel sympathetic about himself, and become blind to the transparency of his realities.

He started to notice when he was invited over for dinner, that it was the first time his friend's family communicated with each other the entire day.

Even his impression of a perfect home had imperfections.

After seeing the lifestyle of his peers who had the hologram of a perfect home, Frank noticed that although he was poor on the outside, he was mentally richer than his peers with parents who were financially free.

Mother Carrie wanted to change the environment that surrounded Frank on a daily basis, so she transferred him to another school. It was further away from where they lived, and it gave him a different view of going to school. He was around more multi-cultural kids and his teachers actually cared about him. Yet, his past life continued to follow him around a like a shadow attempting to contaminate his new environment.

In the midst of his high school years, Frank encountered one near brush with the law in an attempt to fit in with his fellow peers. His closest friend decided to steal merchandise from a store, and it wasn't the best friend who brought it to Frank's attention. Policemen stopped them and for the simple fact that Frank was seen on camera walking around with him, they questioned him like he committed the crime as well. This was a defining moment; because in the process of being interrogated for a crime he didn't commit, he transitioned from a follower to a leader.

Ever since his encounter with the law that he didn't orchestrate, he walked in fear of doing the wrong thing. He tip-toed in fear because he didn't want the law to define him in a bitter way. He didn't want to be labeled as someone he wasn't with characteristics he didn't possess; with his mugshot as the cover to a story that wasn't true. He refused to let the law tattoo their own perception of him across his forehead.

This small interrogation window within one's conscience is where millions of people fail to listen until it's too late. When you grow up without an identity of who you truly are, you tend to stop by the wrong lunch tables in an attempt to fit in and finally have an identity. The world doesn't tell you early on that the mainstream current your flesh wishes to fit into is a current that will take you further away from your sole purpose in life.

It's the world vs your legacy and when you differentiate between the two, you'll get a clear perspective on the priorities and sacrifices that must be made in order to stay the course. Otherwise, you'll veer off course later down the road of life.

You can get tricked by trying to fit into the world especially when you already have a disoriented legacy. If your family is generationally lost and you try to fit into the world, you'll become more lost and eventually lose everything you have.

Some people change who they are for things that are worldly. However, if you know what's best for your family legacy, then trying to fit in would never cross your mind. Organizations fight for you to gain access to knowledge but after you get access there's another problem. You must be careful once you get a degree and break poverty because merely fitting into mainstream isn't your purpose. You could actually graduate college and go backwards!

Purpose is bigger than waking up...making money...and fitting into America.

Make sure your degree is adjacent to your purpose because college can steal from your family legacy as well. Research the numbers of what your degree will bring per year because it takes a toll on people who cannot find a job afterwards. College isn't for everyone because it gives you access to debt if it's not defined in your purpose.

Frank was a C average student in high school. He didn't struggle in school because he didn't focus on the system as it presented itself. He didn't plan on attending college because school only bridged the gap to a few of his circumstances. School gave him access to an extra meal each day, social interaction, and core elements of his self-development.

You can become distracted by the image of what the school system should and shouldn't do for you; because it's impossible for academics to define who you truly are.

If you were to transition your thought patterns and focus on fighting for the legacy of your family, you would march against the current of mainstream America.

Chapter 10

Discipline or Death

"In the free fall of faith, I almost fell to my fate; I got so close to seeing death I got a glimpse of the gates."

Since Frank lacked a father who provided guidance throughout his life, he felt he was walking down a self-inflicted suicidal path after high school. At the time, this destructive route was the only path he saw. Neither his mother nor anyone else around their home could grant him the discipline needed to survive after high school.

His high school diploma gave him access to the real world, but he automatically knew he wasn't fit to survive. He felt he didn't have any skill sets relevant to any jobs in the work force. During his childhood and adolescent years, all he knew was how to eat, sleep, and breathe into existence what it took to take care of his family... not himself.

He found himself at the fork in the road between discipline and death. Discipline was a characteristic vital to his survival but did not exist in his upbringing. So, he turned to the one place where discipline would always outweigh the uncertainty camping on his conscience... the U.S. Military.

The journey to your treasure is packed with defining moments. They act like quick-time decisions that pop into your mind like your conscience on both shoulders. One preaches discipline and the other preaches death.

When you know you lack something, you must accept it by choosing discipline. This is the only way to fill the gaps of your vulnerability, so don't be afraid to speak into it.

You are choosing death if you don't and your ignorance will outweigh your intelligence if you continue to ignore it.

Please don't give the ignorance in your imagination the ability to define you during these pivotal moments in your life. You don't have to know everything, but you do need a presentation about yourself that allows successful individuals to want to pour more into you. You will not erase your vulnerabilities by faking it till you make it like the world made you think. You get it by being honest with those who have the knowledge to change your life; and expose your vulnerabilities so they can build you up based on the wisdom they have.

His branch of choice was the U.S. Army. He felt it was the only branch that would accept him without highlighting his academics. He focused more on providing for his family instead of spending time studying and earning the best grades he could in school.

He signed on the dotted line confirming the risk he was willing to take. He didn't fear for his life when he left for the military. However, Mother Carrie was filled with fear because none of her children had ever been that far away from her umbrella of security.

When Frank left for the military, Mother Carrie was a nervous wreck. She thought she had lost her world. Frank was the one who took care of their family and she feared the thought that he might not return.

Mother Carrie still supported her son's decision; because she believed in his vision although she couldn't see it in high definition from a single mother's perspective.

The biggest gift Belinda gave her brother was the security of eliminating the evils of the world he never saw, because they couldn't survive beyond her defensive barrier. She sacrificed scholarships to stay home and take care of Mother Carrie. Regardless of the cost; Belinda didn't allow anything to disrupt her brother's tunnel vision for their family legacy.

He was stationed at Hunter Airfield in Savannah, Georgia. He was assigned to the 24th Infantry Division. His group trained for instances where their deployment unit assisted when reinforcements were needed.

His team went to Fort Greely in Alaska, and 29 Palms in California to train as a deployment unit. This was the transition that forced fear into his military career. He feared for his life because he understood that anything could happen at any given point in time since he was part of a deployment unit. After enduring bad weather training in Alaska, it isolated his mind from what he was used to seeing; because the moon and sun switched places every three months instead of every day.

Frank was surrounded by the company of his unit, but he felt the vibrations of loneliness echoing in the trenches of his soul.

He wrote letters to his mother in an attempt to appease his internal loneliness, hoping that the safety net from home would capture it before drifting out of reach. This was the moment when for the first time he and his mother exchanged phrases like

"I miss you…"

and "I love you," although this wasn't how his family was accustomed to communicating with each other.

Frank wasn't attracted to any specific leaders while in the military. He gravitated towards the leadership in general that the military kept in place. He departed the army after three years of service because his main objective in the military was discipline and structure. He received an honorable discharge, but his most cherished award came while on active duty...the discipline he originally yearned for.

He was awarded the discipline of how to survive in his home country, as a token of appreciation for serving his country.

Unfortunately, he found himself disoriented once he returned home. He didn't know exactly where his life was going but he still brought maximum security home from the military.

A real, full grown man was finally in his mother's home, but most importantly he was still alive.

Chapter 11

Ambition worth Millions

"When you race this fast money, don't crash into the ditches; it's so much roadkill on this road to riches."

After serving three years in the military, Frank had two job offers on the table when he returned home to Milwaukee. One was at a financial institution and the other was in the automotive industry.

He yearned to work in an industry that didn't have any limits, and could give him the opportunity to self-create the longevity of his career. He accepted the offer in the automotive industry. He was hired as a salesperson at the Heiser Lincoln Mercury dealership in Milwaukee, Wisconsin. His personal goal in this job was to sell so much that he became oblivious to the limits in his mind, and feed off his unlimited potential.

Frank was inspired by the owner of the dealership who hired him, an Italian business owner named Mr. Scafitti.

Frank felt honored when he first met Mr. Scafitti. He was another leader who valued him for lacking guidance, and knew Frank would be more effective in life if he patched the open wounds from his past. Mr. Scafitti was purposefully hard on Frank. He knew he would chisel his skills into a diamond if he applied the right amount of pressure. Eventually, this pressure burst the pipes of Frank's potential and blew his mind!

Frank excelled in his position as a salesperson. He started selling over thirty vehicles in a short period of time, like it was normal for someone his age to rack up such numbers. His customers naturally gravitated to him because he was truthful, transparent, and credible.

Even with early success, his boss was so hard on him that tears were summoned in Frank's reflection. He felt like he had let him down. Mr. Scafitti removed the mask that was a requirement to the survival of his status, revealing the seed he planted through the transparency of Frank's character.

Mr. Scafitti told Frank,

"I'm hard on you because I love you, and I think you're going to be pretty good. I can see things in you that you cannot see right now."

These words from his boss gave him access to something his ears had never heard before. The transparency of these truthful words unlocked a secret in Frank's mind… love can exist in the business world. He understood relationships with successful individuals would build a bridge in the direction of his purpose. The foundation of Frank's strength was giving his mentors access to building his character. Each brick laid was strong enough to hold an empire.

There are people who cross your path specifically designed for a task. Start to understand what that purpose is and stay within those boundaries. This is how you gain access to the next steps on your mission to locating your treasure.

One evening while Frank was working, he saw an individual walk into the dealership dressed for success in the sharpest suit he had ever seen. His name was Emile Banks and he had come to purchase a vehicle from Frank. Mr. Banks was an assistant pastor at a local church. Frank wanted access to his character because he sensed the leadership he carried beyond the boundaries of his flesh.

Let these individuals activate the compass in your mind with the magnetic pull of the right direction.

He built a mentoring relationship with Mr. Banks and was later introduced to the head pastor of Mr. Banks' church, Bishop Darrell Hines. Frank received spiritual guidance from Mr. Hines and learned the character of a man from Mr. Banks. Although he wanted to know everything about these two major influencers in his life, he never got too close because he didn't want to view them from the perspective of their flesh. He knew if he got too up close and personal it would've made him judgmental, and he would've become blind to the blessings they were planting into his life.

Spiritually, mentally, and physically...Frank had upgraded from a boy to a man. A real man of flesh and bone.

Did Mr. Scafiti hurt your feelings?

Hint:

Their constructive criticism cut you into a diamond; but you became a professional because they forced you to polish yourself.

Chapter 12

Flesh over Future

"When you feed your flesh, you starve your future."

Frank felt like had had finally become the man he was supposed to be, but one thing was still missing in his life… a wife.

He met two women around the same time and found himself wavering between who he wanted to pursue. One of these beautiful ladies was established and spent most of her time working and investing in her future. The other lady was drop dead gorgeous and spent most of her time fueling the flame of a life that was socially exciting!

Frank never gave himself permission to have a social life, because he grew up with tunnel vision. Putting food on the table for his family was the only image that gave him life on a daily basis. Since he never had the opportunity to adopt an exciting social life, he thought this is what had been missing in his own world. He chose his Cinderella based solely on who could give him the missing puzzle piece that was socially exciting. This flame was controlled by a woman named Desiree.

His relationship with Desiree was beyond the boundaries of excitement. He felt like he was exploring a whole new world filled with everything he missed growing up, but amplified on a whole new level. They were attracted to every party like a moth to a flame; dove head-first into every alcoholic beverage poured before them; and Desiree mastered the art of bringing Frank's wildest fantasies into reality.

Frank and Desiree spent so many nights on the town that their nightlife became brighter than the morning sun.

There are consequences to an unconditional love and he never understood the knowledge of what love really meant. Since excitement was the only flame being fueled in their relationship, these consequences started haunting Frank like a ghost in the shade of his shadow.

He disappeared into the nightlife and almost lost sight of who he originally set himself out to be. He explored the uncharted territories of his excitement with Desiree as his tour guide every step of the way.

He had an accelerated plunge to rock bottom because he fell in love too fast. He was attracted to what fed his flesh and physically made him feel good. He thought he filled the gap in his upbringing with the correct person. He soon realized that there were missing puzzle pieces scattered across the board of his life and he had accidentally stepped where pieces had not been placed.

Desiree and Frank were good hearted people. However, they lacked the characteristics of knowledge, maturity, and stability that were the heartbeat to a life-long relationship.

After getting their first apartment together, they mentally adopted an expectation for a future they never stopped to feed. Their social life was always present in the moment and happy to be alive! However, the longevity of their relationship had already starved to death.

Their previous lifestyle created a black hole in their bank account. They didn't notice at first because it was camouflaged with the nightlife. Their relationship was dysfunctional and when things became tough financially, Desiree threatened that she would leave Frank.

Desiree pacified the weaknesses within him that came from being a fatherless child.

When you're at your most vulnerable, you attract things that make you feel better but aren't necessarily what's best for you. Desiree represented a weakness within Frank, something that existed before they even met each other. He had to find the heartbeat of Desiree's existence within himself so he could remove the flame which she was attracted to.

Just when he thought there wasn't room for anymore struggles in his life, there was a tiny feather that broke the camel's back... a positive pregnancy test.

Frank and Desiree were expecting a child. Frank felt important when he first found out but also scared. Once again, he lacked the road map of what something else meant in his life. It was another responsibility that he didn't have an identification for. He feared that he would approach it the wrong way because he didn't know how to develop a strong relationship with a female. Working, paying bills, and bringing food home was all he knew.

He found himself incarcerated in a self-made conundrum. He didn't know how to handle the struggles he'd absorbed into the orbit of his life.

Do you have a Desiree?

Hint:

They're not necessarily a bad person, but they navigate with a broken compass.

Chapter 13

Cupid's Unconditional Arrow

"Regardless of how many wrinkles I get, my love will never grow old."

On September 28, 1989, his daughter Anastasia was born.

Frank's relationship with Desiree was already stumbling off course, so he feared that he would accidentally guide his daughter the wrong way. He jumped into the corner of the room when asked to cut Stacy's umbilical cord. He became petrified of the new challenge at hand.

Stacy's birth was the moment he recognized the responsibility to change the legacy of his thoughts, perspectives, and life in general. The next generation of his family tree had sprouted, and he didn't want to pass on the generational curses he was forced to grow up with. Stacy literally gave him access to the best version of himself. A true, living, breathing, present father!

Although he didn't have the knowledge of how to raise Stacy the right way at first; he was still overprotective just like Mother Carrie was with him.

His relationship with Desiree became toxic after Stacy was born. They were stumbling on a thin line between being socially exciting as a couple and raising a child the correct way as parents; they couldn't find the balance.

He failed in the process of trying to keep things afloat for his relationship with Desiree. He was trying to understand how to upgrade the maturity in the relationship, but no time had been invested in laying this foundation. It was something that would have been a dual investment on both sides, and Desiree's expectations from Frank were high as a skyscraper.

People will attempt to make you feel like you're the problem when in reality the relationship simply wasn't mature. It became impossible to withstand what it took to raise a child the correct way.

Frank didn't feel any pressure dealing with his five-year-old Stacy. Everything he wanted to change for her felt like the real missing puzzle piece that he originally thought Desiree would give him. It was the first time he loved someone unconditionally and she transformed his entire life.

Stacy was a fierce little girl, and she fueled the flame that brightened Frank's world.

Are you a good role model for the Stacy's you haven't met?

Hint:

They look up to you, want to be just like you, and love you unconditionally regardless of what you do.

Chapter 14

Broken Shackles

"Mental breakdowns are the breaking points
where you can make a breakthrough."

Desiree reached the climax of her breaking point and decided to break up with Frank. His heart was broken for the first time and his soul bled from every shard of their shattered memories.

The thought of someone quitting on him was one of his biggest fears in life. Ever since he was eight years old, he thought his happiness only existed in his ability to provide. After Desiree broke up with Frank, he moved back home with Mother Carrie. He was convicted by the pressures of being a young individual with the responsibility of serving. He soon realized that he never had a chance to truly enjoy life.

Catastrophic thoughts start to form like dark clouds when you have no one mentally relieving you from these pressures.

His mind flooded from the precipitation of these dark thoughts forcing him to feel like he no longer had a purpose in life. Since the mother of his child shined a spotlight on his darkest fear, his conscience whispered,

"Your purpose has expired," so he interrogated his existence and contemplated suicide.

Frank locked himself in his old room mentally set on taking his life…

He gave his reflection in the mirror the death stare and took a deep breath. One disoriented individual, one broken heart - generationally cursed by confusion with one in the chamber. His legacy trembled on a flatline because he thought his life's relevance had met its deadline.

The legacy of Frank J. Williams was about to exhale its last breath of existence…However, one little girl was 100% sure his life still had relevance.

Suicidal thoughts knocking on his skull were interrupted by Stacy's little knock on his door. He heard his daughter say,

"Daddy?" and a seed of hope was planted in the soil of his suicidal thoughts.

Stacy gave him access to the most pivotal point in his life and legacy. Without her unconditional love for her daddy, he would've never transformed into the best version of himself. He now wanted different instead of only doing different.

He didn't commit suicide physically; however, he did commit suicide mentally. Stacy revealed to him blessings that come from freeing yourself from your old ways and single perspective insights. It was originally a nightmare, but sunshine came in the morning.

Broken people live in broken homes. There's healthiness of transparency in a broken home, and the cure is understanding that suicide and depression is a natural thing.

The world slaps a negative label on people who are suffering from suicide and depression. However, these are merely the side effects from the developmental stages taking place. This window of self-grief is your opportunity to pinpoint the treasures you want in life; so you'll cherish everything you now live for. This molds you into becoming a stronger individual. When you are brought to your knees from a mental breakdown don't forget to claim your breakthrough. It's a collapse and reconstruction.

People who are walking under an umbrella of depression don't understand how powerful the raindrops from their dark clouds really are. When you harness the confidence that's hidden among these clouds in your mind, it'll reveal the powerful characteristics in yourself that are blessings once disguised as negative viewpoints. Depression will no longer force you to give up on yourself during your defining moments. It won't make you look at your own reflection as merely a race. You'll finally accept the blessings you once believed you didn't deserve that have been waiting on your doorstep. Also, you'll understand that where you are in this moment is merely temporary, but it was necessary for the survival of your legacy.

Chapter 15

My Angel's Pandora Box

"Every failure is your maturity
opportunity."

Frank was learning how to gain strength for himself so he could climb out of the trenches that were the lowest parts of his life.

His relationship with Desiree sunk because he accepted the role of a man even though he wasn't fully educated on the logistics of how a real man operates. He only was a man by age, appearance, sex and bringing money home. Until an angel named Trinity flew into his world and filled the gaps in his upbringing with three sets of blessings.

Trinity was a stable woman with a strong personality. He approached Trinity with caution based on the experience gained from his previous relationship. He didn't want to repeat the same scene over again. Frank loved her to death, but she scared him more than anything at the same time. She frightened him because she actually took care of him. He couldn't figure out why any woman would love him unconditionally when he originally lacked so much. Another reason her love caught him off guard was because he was used to taking care of himself. He had never experienced someone loving him on such a level.

The first set of blessings Trinity gave him included knowledge and wisdom in the empty areas of his life.

She nurtured areas of his life that no woman had ever visited before. She satisfied a gap that even his mother couldn't fill. She blessed him with endless amounts of unconditional love as well as giving him a different perspective on family due to the togetherness of her own family. Trinity continued to mature as a woman while Frank still struggled with his transition into manhood. However, she still nurtured him in every area she could.

When you go from having no one love you to someone flooding you with affection, it'll scare you at first. The lack in your previous relationships will make you feel like you don't deserve this person.

The second set of blessings Trinity gave him included wedding rings, and knowledge on how to co-parent with Desiree since he didn't have custody of Anastasia.

Frank was very uncertain of where his future with Trinity would go if he continued to lack knowledge; so, they both attended marriage counseling to polish their relationship to the best of their ability.

They had a pastor give them guidance on marriage so they could strengthen their stability. Also, they were given the ability to learn what sacrifice, commitment, and marriage really meant. Marriage counseling was contagious to Frank, because it was giving him answers to so many things a father was never there to tell him.

Men can do things like this early in their relationship with a woman they want a future with. It'll break fatherless chains that have been shackling their family down for generations. If nobody in your family has ever been married and you continue to marry based on lack of knowledge, then your honeymoon might be a trip to divorce court.

If you prepare yourself prior to marriage, you'll get the truth of how to become whole and it becomes easier to accept the person you're meant to be with. It'll help men tap into their wives' natural instincts. They'll learn how to harness their emotions instead of hurting them from a series of misunderstandings.

Although Frank was once a mistake in the making, he always yearned for ways to fill the gaps in his life that were never nurtured. He was Trinity's pandora box because his life was flooded with mistakes. There was still a small spec of hope swimming in the puddle of his past tears, and it forever shapeshifted the future of his family legacy.

Have you found your Trinity?

Hint:

They're a reflection of your soul and are in love with your passion; but loved you enough to not rush into a relationship.

Chapter 16

Seed of Purpose

"I sprouted without a dad. So, it's my responsibility to give you the father I never had."

The third set of blessings Trinity gave Frank included a small seed at the bottom of the box... The thought of having a son.

Frank knew from the beginning that he wanted his son to be a Jr. because he wanted to continue the legacy that originally sprouted from his childhood trauma.

Stacy gave him access to being more prepared because before she was born, he was dysfunctional without the image of how to raise a child correctly. Stacy forced him to understand the blessing of life. He yearned for a son so he could recreate himself; and give a variation of himself the father he never had.

Frank and Trinity both knew Frank Jr. was destined to be special, because he was brought into the world through in vitro fertilization.

Trinity no longer had the ability to reproduce on her own. The process of in vitro fertilization was a sacrifice she endured. It was a higher level of commitment Frank had never seen before, so it was gratifying from his perspective.

Growing up fatherless was the resource he used to outline what to instill in his son, so he could grow up the complete opposite way.

His son Frankie is the gift of GOD he felt he didn't deserve.

It felt surreal to him that he felt less bothered by growing up without a father when he first saw Frankie the moment he was born. His excuse had transformed into another real-life responsibility. He named him Frank Jr. because legacy was growing in his mind and spirit. He looked at life from the perspective of what he was going to accomplish. He believed that his son would be proud to carry a name that will play a part in paving a new foundation for the world.

Even when a father is in a child's life, there are still things a father cannot teach his son. Things like what his purpose is, what he accepts it to be, and what he wants of life for himself. These cannot come from his parents!

However, a father can provide guidance at the holes he cannot fill. He can teach his son the importance of himself and what he believes in.

Teach your children how to write it, look for it, and start to identify what makes them happy beyond their flesh. Teach them not to be afraid of what their life and legacy looks like! Teach them how not to view their blessings as if they don't deserve them. This is how you ensure they'll never settle for less; and later in life won't go through a series of a million relationships to finally find the right one.

Frank wasn't taught these things early because his father wasn't in his life and his mother simply didn't know. This was because generational poverty was so deeply rooted in his family at that time.

At a young age, Frankie saw that his father was an extremely hard worker but didn't fully understand why. Frankie played sports growing up and noticed his father sometimes missed some of his ball games. However, the games he did attend, he would name a list of things for Frankie to improve on even though he had a great game. He was always hard on Frankie, because he was mentally preparing him for the family legacy he would one day become the designated pilot for.

Frankie grew up watching his father work around the dealerships. He asked his father what he planned on doing in the future. He told Frankie that he wanted to build a family legacy and he was part of that blueprint by design.

Frank didn't want the curses from his generational poverty to become hereditary with his son. He kept them from becoming hand me downs by planting in his son what was originally a missing puzzle piece for himself. He taught his son at a young age to always respect women but always...always look at himself first to make sure he was whole before considering someone else.

Have you prepared your Frankie for the next level?

Hint:

They will one day carry your torch and take it to heights that were once out of sight.

Chapter 17

Frank Williams vs. the Battle on Homefront

"The fight against generational poverty is a series of battles amongst your own blood."

Frank didn't realize the importance of being in a child's life on a direct basis until his son was living with him...but his daughter Stacy wasn't.

Belinda reminded him that he needed to get full custody of Stacy so she wouldn't become a statistic of Desiree's poverty driven environment. He transitioned this situation onto Belinda mostly because he didn't know exactly how to approach it based on his past with Desiree.

This was the moment Frank realized that it takes more than one person to retrieve a family legacy correctly. Everyone had to be on their cues.

Belinda's backbone was strong enough to hold the weight of things on the responsible side of their family legacy. Frank entrusted Belinda with his world because he knew she was strong enough to hold it.

He knew Belinda would allow him to stay focused on his tunnel vision of bringing his family blessings they never would have imagined.

Stacy was in Desiree's custody living in an environment where generational poverty was once again deeply rooted. While on the opposite side of the fence; Frank was in the process of building the legacy of real fathers in his family.

Stacy lacked the father that Frankie had access to on a daily basis. Desiree was once Frank's kryptonite, but he was finally becoming stronger as a real father and understood the measures of where he had to go for the future of his children. He fought through court and made financial sacrifices to win custody of Anastasia. Now, he finally had both of his biological children in the legacy driven environment he was building.

He was a little intimidated going through the process of getting custody of his daughter. He was in his mid-twenties, and the court system had a scary atmosphere when you're oblivious of what the outcome to your case might be.

Frank had a scar on his arm from boiling hot water when he was a kid. It was a reminder of what a man is capable of doing to an innocent woman based on what he saw Mother Carrie endure that night. He now fully understood the fear of emptiness and security he witnessed his mother struggle with. His biggest fears for his daughter wasn't the knowledge he lacked like in his son's case. He feared her exposure to poverty in the images she was bound to see under Desiree's roof.

After getting custody of Stacy, both of his children sensed they were dramatically different from one another. There was always a constant battle of jealousy. One seed planted properly while the other one wasn't. Stacy came from a broken environment, but Frankie didn't. There was a clash between both cultures since they didn't understand each other at first.

As a child, Stacy felt like she was the only soldier fighting a series of battles. These battles were amongst her environment and the fear of having no one in her corner. Her life was bipolar in nature. She had to uphold the fundamentals of survival in Desiree's poverty driven neighborhood, but things were completely opposite within the boundaries of Frank's legacy driven home.

Stacy spent more time around Belinda's son, Kevin Lee Jr. because he played a pivotal role as her emotional safety net…

just like Belinda was for Frank.

Stacy also noticed that her father was an extremely hard worker. He would be gone by the time she woke up in the morning and didn't get home till later in the evening when she was already in bed for the night. She understood that a man in America was either at home and not financially stable, or financially stable but not home with the family much. It took her a while to grasp the fact that this was the reality of her situation with her father.

Stacy could have easily become the statistic society claimed she would be while growing up on 19th & Hampton in Milwaukee, Wisconsin. She would have gravitated in the wrong direction if not for her auntie Belinda.

In Stacy's new legacy driven environment, she learned that legacy is what allows your name to still ring a bell in the minds of people after you're dead and gone, because you still hold weight in the world. It took her time to understand what her father was doing for them. When it clicked in her mind, she was thankful for her father being the most selfless person she knew. She adopted this characteristic from her father which was passed to him from Mother Carrie.

While Frank had custody of Stacy, he was only able to keep her for a certain number of days per month. It scared him knowing she was going back into the wilderness of poverty when she was out of his reach.

He was functioning as a real father in front of his children. Yet, he never stopped to explain that although they are siblings, they came from two different worlds in his process of breaking poverty in their family tree.

Chapter 18

Price of Legacy

*"The price you're willing to pay is the price
to break the curse."*

There was a point in time when Frank was starting
to get his first taste of major success in the
automotive industry.... However, he was still of the
world.

He was becoming extremely successful but forgot
to practice saving and investing.

Frank invested a lot into tithes and offerings at
his church. He asked Emile Banks and Bishop Darrell
Hines if he could have a portion of it back to have
funds for Christmas.

He felt close enough to them to be comfortable
making such a request. However, they both refused
him because it simply wasn't the right thing to do.

This was the moment Frank started focusing
more on practicing how to save and invest years into
the future. He worked extremely hard for an entire
year giving both Mr. Banks and Mr. Hines a check for
the exact amount he requested from them a year

prior. He did this gesture because he understood that he was still of the world when he asked them for the money.

His spirit was originally in the wrong place; but he paid the exact price to make his wrongful spirit right.

In the process of doing so he learned how to save and invest correctly. He also learned more about what he lacked as a man and how to fill those gaps himself.

Did you think the Mr. Banks in your life wasn't going to test you?

Hint:

They haven't challenged you yet; but they love you, so don't be surprised when they do.

Chapter 19

Christmas Gifts Galore

"I used to walk by faith but now I execute by faith."

When you execute by faith you actually walk out and get major things done. This was the moment Frank became a major gap filler for his community.

Executing by faith has a higher trust level required in order to get things accomplished. When Frank understood that GOD was speaking to him and He was being truthful…it scared him to the point that he felt the need to seek spiritual guidance once again. He knew things would manifest if he simply stayed the course following the plan GOD revealed unto him, but the fear came from a lack of understanding on a cosmic scale.

When you work for people, leaders, and take care of a family, you'll get the impression that your responsibilities are mapped out the way the world says you should do things. However, you have to create an ethical way of doing the things assigned only to you.

Frank understood he had to do things differently in the business world to survive and remain successful. He got baptized twice in an attempt to gain an extra layer of spiritual protection.

He asked GOD to guide him in the business world when he stepped into the water for the second time, because he didn't understand how to navigate leadership.

From a worldly perspective, he was taught leadership was all about money, titles, and positions; instead, he studied to become a servant leader in the business world. He learned how to serve as an honest leader who found relevance in his previous mistakes. He learned how they actually brighten the future of his path executed the correct way. He's overly humble, overly grateful, and extremely thankful for the circumstances he grew up in. He learned how to take pride in his upbringing. The humility of where he came from is the greatest testament that keeps him safe.

He started paying it forward on a larger scale. He donated to organizations that were gap fillers for disoriented teens growing up in situations similar to his on a weekly basis. He's always given a natural feeling to serve others in need.

Mother Carrie is the one who instilled this servant mentality in him. He was frustrated as a kid when Mother Carrie freely gave things away. From the perspective of a successful businessman, that was the only reason he knew how to give, donate, and sponsor the correct way. He knew he met who he was supposed to meet and did what he was supposed to do on a larger scale for his community.

Although he became a highly successful individual forced to find his own way; his conscience whispered to him that he should reach out to the one person who didn't know the depth of his success... his biological father.

Chapter 20

Product of a Single Parent Home

"I couldn't say farewell at your funeral, but I'll say it's nice to meet you at the Golden Gates."

Originally, he wanted to reach out to his biological father solely to show him the successful man he turned out to be without him.

He procrastinated in reaching out to his father. The thought came and went on a weekly basis. He never had an understanding on the core reason why his father was never in his life. He wanted his dad to regret not being involved in his life. Also, he felt it was his duty to be the one who was man enough to reach out first.

He reached out to his father but realized he had waited a thought too late. His father Curtis Logan had passed away from diabetes.

He felt a chord in his spirit break when his father passed away. It was a connection he didn't know existed inside himself. He regretted not reaching out to his father sooner. Based on his original reason, he wasn't sure if it was for the best or worse...

His father was cremated, and he didn't get a chance to see him. His father had married a woman who wasn't going to grant him access to view him.

The wounds that came from growing up without his father started to bleed internally. He missed the window of opportunity to change the origins of his legacy.

You might grow up fatherless, but you'll always have GOD, your Heavenly Father on your side. You're in control of the narrative that speaks to the gifts inside you. You must understand that the battles are not lost. You can still have access, wealth, and everything you ever yearned for...even if it's always been missing.

Is there a Curtis Logan haunting you?

Hint:

You wish you could rewind time, so you could deposit things differently and spend more time.

Chapter 21

Ambition worth Billions

"When you fight for generational wealth, you study the stars till you become one yourself."

F rank worked for the dealership in Milwaukee from 1988 to 2008. He saw a new job opportunity in Automotive News, a newspaper that published updates on what was going on in the automotive industry across the country.

Americas first African American billionaire Robert L. Johnson was forming a company and was in search of partners. When Frank responded to the article, he felt nervous knowing who Robert Johnson was. He couldn't believe there was a chance he could play a role in a vision so vast. He reached for the stars because he knew he had the skill sets needed for one of the positions.

Frank stepped foot in an interview with the most powerful president and vice president in the automotive industry, Steve Landers and Franklin McLarty. They served as representation for Bob Johnson and Mack McLarty.

When Frank spoke in the interview with Steve Landers and Franklin McLarty, they didn't meet an adult. They met a magnified version of who Frank was as an eight-year old.

Based on his skill set, he got the job as part owner and operator of Landers McLarty in Huntsville, Alabama. He also had the opportunity to later meet Bob Johnson and Mack McLarty.

He felt like he had met one of the most important men in the world when he met Bob Johnson. He had to slow himself down when he met him although there was a lot of excitement and anticipation, so he could grasp the principles of how to navigate under the tutorage of billionaires.

The sermon of great business in Bob's character stood out the most to Frank. He quickly noticed that he was a critical thinker on a higher level. He had to quickly adopt this same confidence that seemed so out of this world, because there wasn't anything emotional in Bob's speech pattern.

Both Frank and Bob had a significant characteristic in common; the passion of giving poverty driven individuals access to the economic system in America. They gave people access by providing platforms.

Although Bob is a billionaire, he didn't give Frank a single penny. He gave him the platform and Frank worked it out at the highest level he possibly could.

He had to come to grips that he was walking out his purpose. He had the opportunity to establish excellence at his first dealership and now he was being interviewed by some of the most powerful people in the world. They were yearning for individuals who had the same skill sets he mastered over time... He didn't find them, they found him!

He knew he was in the presence of a legacy driven individual when he met Mack McLarty. He had to quickly understand the purpose of every single word said in the conversation. Mack McLarty is one of the most astute businessmen he ever met, who harnessed the temperament of an icon.

Frank was honored to meet Robert L. Johnson and Mack McLarty; not because of their net worth but because they both have family legacies.

Chapter 22

A Frank Williams Dealership

"When you give yourself permission to accept the truth, you give the next generation permission to heal, grow, and carry the torch."

In 2008, Frank was hired as owner and operator of Landers McLarty in Huntsville, Alabama; and moved his family down south with him.

He came to Huntsville completely oblivious of the impact he would have on his new community. As of today, Frank Williams is part owner/operator of four franchises.

Belinda is beyond thankful for the man her brother represents. He's a man who's humble, caring, and wears his heart on his sleeve. Her brother was driven and always gravitated towards the successful people around him. It's very humbling knowing where they came from. She knew at a young age that her brother would accomplish something major and she would be an essential part of that legacy.

Belinda is the one who cycles the wrong people out of his peripheral vision, even in his business world. If anyone was to harm him, they would automatically harm a community of people who depend on him. As long as she's blessed to breathe, no one will come into their family and destroy it. To destroy their family is to destroy the generations coming after them. Protection was the greatest gift Mother Carrie could've possibly given her. That's where she adopted the security of how to protect her brother on the level he grew to be. The transition to his son wouldn't have been successful without her security being present in the environment. She hopes there is something about her that they can carry on as a reference to help someone else.

When you're around someone who has a family legacy, what you learn from them can become the greatest education in the world.

Money can pacify some aspects of life, but it cannot buy legacy spiritually or emotionally. Some people don't understand the power they have equipped with the talents they possess. When they use it the wrong way, they sometimes do a society of people an injustice.

A family legacy is true when everyone within the family continues to build each other up physically, mentally, spiritually, emotionally, and financially. They need to be in sync at all times.

When Frank looks at his reflection every day, he still feels as though his mission isn't over. He thinks there is much more that GOD wants him to execute by faith upon. These thoughts are not equipped with stress because they are reminders of why he needs to continue being a good servant; and water what Mother Carrie planted in him as a child.

Since he's no longer of the world, he doesn't see himself as someone who's well off or making a lot of money.

We all can make a difference in the world on a great level. It's not merely redirecting the paradigm of poverty in our family, because our source of relevance is so much bigger than ourselves.

His unspoken obligations started to become overwhelming to him. He learned how to pace himself when executing by faith. This is how he is most efficient without getting anxiety.

He held on tight to the integrity of Frank Williams in cursive that he had written over and over again as a child. His legacy is an identification of the blood, sweat, tears, and erased fears in his unfortunate upbringing. Originally, he thought it would be money, but it wasn't. It was the little things like writing his name in cursive when it lacked an identity and meant nothing through the eyes of the world. His signature was destined to mean more than he could ever imagine.

He now wants to experience and connect life the correct way. This gave him access to the legacy he strives for today. His biggest goal at Landers McLarty in Huntsville is to create a line of dealerships that illustrate his legacy even after he's gone. He plans on passing the torch to Frankie so he can pick up where he leaves off; then their legacy can be taken to the next level that only his son has the purpose to continue.

Frankie is most thankful for the hard work and dedication his father instilled in him. He watched his father grow and noticed that he doesn't do things for himself. He sees the bigger picture and strives to make everyone in his circumference successful as well.

Frankie understood that legacy isn't something built in a year, but a daily investment in order to be eligible for the next generation. His father educated him on not being materialistic, and how to think about what's going to have an effect on his life ten years down the road.

A family legacy isn't designed for only the current living family, the blueprint outlines how it'll gradually be carried on for hundreds of years.

Your family legacy will hold a culture to itself with consistency. Even when you're gone, your legacy will serve as a foundation.

Chapter 23

Legacy Letters in Cursive

*"Your experiences don't curse you.... they
define the legacy that's in you."*

Frank always wanted to change the dynamics of
his mother raising children in poverty. Mother
Carrie gave him access to the fuel that will drive their
family legacy for generations. She gave him
preparation by giving him a reflection of what his
life's picture was. They lived in poverty their entire
life eating one meal a day off of food stamps. They
didn't have access to anything with the exception of
images poverty promoted before them. His life's
struggle turned out to be the depth of his generational
legacy.

He always wanted to continue preparing and
doing better for his kids because his fight had never
been about himself.

Originally, he was going to give his son a
financial gift when he graduated from college...the
traditional graduation gift in America.

However, he realized that a financial gift would merely be temporary and lack long-term purpose if Frank Jr. never knew his father's truths.

This is when he discovered the missing treasure in America...

It was one thing he never had, the benefits of a father who talked to him in the aspect of life.

Is the valedictorian's speech really heard if one does not receive a speech of truth from their own parents first?

He wanted Frankie to understand his specific role in their family legacy by both thanking him and releasing him before the people who loved him most. He couldn't think of a more perfect time to tell his children what he truly wanted to say to them. He knew it would mean the world if recited at his son's graduation celebration.

He knew if he said it publicly it would release him from the burdens of his curses, so his son could properly contribute to the next generation of their family legacy. He wanted his children to know both the good and the regrets of his life while watching them grow up.

He wanted to transfer generational legacy from father to son, correctly.

At first, he would have given his son the same cycle of what his legacy was fueled from. However, his son's legacy is destined to be different because Frankie had to master the responsibilities of being a good steward.

He wanted to write letters to his children as graduation gifts, and address the truth of their father that they never knew. He wanted his son to understand that Daddy had some things but also lacked simultaneously. This grants Frankie the opportunity to fill the gaps his father couldn't, because he fought a completely different battle. A father figure once never existed but now his family tree will have a legacy of fathers.

However, Stacy was the key that granted their family tree access to its generational legacy.

Heirloom of Truth

Dear Frank Jr.

"My true legacy was always you too, Frankie."

December 15, 2018

Dear Frank Jr.

I know you had a front row seat throughout your life watching me fight against the poverty deeply rooted in our family tree. However, your college graduation is the first time I've had the opportunity to see my legacy in high definition. I know you desired the extra father-son moments from me but in order to establish the foundation you stand on today I had to sacrifice those memories in exchange for your purposeful future.

My biggest fear in life was the thought of you walking out the door every day without a father directing you at the forks in the road on this journey called life. I need you to accept the fact that I did lack some things. It wasn't my purpose to be everything because I lacked a father who could navigate me through life; and provide a road map for me to show you all the correct routes. Take the moments I couldn't give you and transfer those dreams into reality. You have the opportunity to harness everything I couldn't be. I want to say thank you for accepting your role and walking it out at the highest level with integrity, credibility, and transparency. I'm proud of the man you have become with the character you possess.

There was once a time I could only dream of this moment, but your sister brought it into reality. I need you to understand that Anastasia is the one who gave you access to everything you know, not me. Poverty was once uncharted territory in our family, but Anastasia motivated me to dig up those roots. Anastasia grew up with the pain from the transition. It was her unconditional love during the healing process that gave me a road map to raise you the right way.

Due to the version of Daddy Anastasia was forced to grow up with, I never gave myself permission to love myself. If you love yourself and never sway from the love you deserve, you'll stay the course and dodge the distractions your father once fell for. If you finish carving the trail I started, you'll find the missing puzzle piece that will complete what the next generation of our legacy needs to be.

Accept this truth as the torch that needs to be taken to the next level. Learn to love yourself before you love someone else; change the trend of fatherhood in our family; and update our legacy with everything you saw from standing on my shoulders.

My true legacy was always you too Frankie,

Love, Dad

Heirloom of Truth

Dear Anastasia

"My true legacy was always you too, Stacy."

December 15, 2018

Dear Anastasia,

I'm sorry I didn't attend your sports and events the way I attended Frank Jr.'s. I missed some defining moments. I did it completely wrong and you deserved that piece of your father as well. I know there were times you may have been bitter towards Frank Jr.'s world; but the truth is, he wouldn't be where he is if it wasn't for you allowing Daddy to heal from his fight against generational poverty.

There was once a time when college degrees didn't grow on our family tree. Not until you embarked on your mission for education and obtained a multitude of them. I was so much of a critic that I was blinded by how strong you really were. Your strength to do what your heart desires is your greatest asset.

I tried to point you in a direction that even I didn't know the destination for. I lacked so much as a parent at the time and you took more control over your life than I've ever given you credit for. I respect you for leaving no stone unturned in your life. I apologize for not praising you more knowing the dysfunctional environment you climbed out of. Your father was once dysfunctional as well, but you still loved me unconditionally. I know I hurt you worse by not expressing this earlier. I'm just now seeing our legacy magnified, so I'm noticing things I didn't see before. Although they've been hiding in plain sight this entire time. I apologize for not giving you the proper congratulations you deserve.

Anastasia Francesca Williams, you are the key that gave our family complete access to the legacy being built. You started a life of acceptance during our transition out of poverty. You not only designed our legacy, but you literally saved your Daddy's life. My fight for family legacy started when you were five years old. I fought through court and everything to keep access to you. I want to say thank you for teaching me the depths of what it means to fight for family, purpose, and legacy. I'm proud of all your accomplishments thus far as well as the independence I know you'll grasp in the future.

My true legacy was always you too Stacy,

Love, Dad

Key to the Heist

Finding your purpose in life is like finding lost treasure. If you can identify adversity in your life, then your purpose has been hiding in plain sight.

Are you actually helping your family, or enabling an invisible enemy named generational poverty?

Answer these questions to initiate your legacy heist.

"How can generational poverty be changed by your commitment to your family?"

"How do your mentors play a part in your life?"

"What do you want to see in your family legacy?"

Symphony of Hearts

"To express myself I shout and sing, for I am merely one feather in an angels vast wing."

Love Note: *to my father*

"What's up! I'm happy to hear about the book. I'm happy to be a part of the legacy you've built. I love you for the sacrifices you have made for me and Anastasia. I might not have always agreed with them but I now see exactly why you made them. I can't wait to be more relevant in our legacy. To help build it to the next level and build generational wealth for generations down the line in our family. I want to thank you for all that you've done for me and helping me out. The communication skills between you and I haven't always been there but I can tell that in the past ten years we've both grown as individuals and built our relationship into something one hundred times better than what it used to be. I see the effort you're putting in. I think the biggest lesson you've taught me is that it's bigger than me. I shouldn't always worry about just helping myself but build up the people around me and make life better for them. I'm just happy to have you as my Dad. I wouldn't have wished for anyone else but you to be my Dad. I love you! I can't wait to read the book. I know it'll be a killer book. I know you did it without a blueprint because you didn't have your dad. I cannot resent you for stuff you did when you originally had no clue. It took time for me to understand that. You didn't have anybody showing you how to do it. When you have no idea, you are going to have mistakes and mess ups. They build who you are. I know you wouldn't have missed a beat between us if you could go back with the knowledge of what you know now. I don't resent you for that because you had to learn along the way too."

Frank Williams II

Love Note: *to my father*

"I forgive you. You're a man who's very, very unique. You're a gem and there aren't many like you. There have been so many times I've looked up and said, I'm glad that man is my Dad. You built this legacy and I promise you as I told you a couple of years ago…I promise you I will carry it on. So again… I forgive you; I love you, you're a gem, and this legacy you've built I promise to carry it on."

Anastasia Williams

Love Note: *to my uncle*

"Hey Frank! I want to say that I'm proud of you for all the things you've done, and all the things I've seen you accomplish. You've done an awesome job with everybody in the family. You took care of us, motivated us, and made us all better. I want you to know that you're leaving everything that you've given us in good hands. We're not going to mess anything up. We're going to do everything we can to make sure that your legacy is brought to light, and it's going to keep expanding. I think you've done a great job with your kids'; you raised them, made them Christians, and put them in positions to succeed for the rest of their lives. I think that you won't have to worry about anything, because I'm going to make sure that everything is taken care of. I'm going to step up when I need to step up; and be the crutch when our family needs me to be the crutch. I'm going to do whatever it takes to make sure this legacy stays strong, and continues to be laid brick by brick to be built further and further. This won't be the end; we're going to keep building and go further than you've ever thought. I'm letting you know I'm going to play a hand in that, and it won't be a small one, I promise I'm going to be a big part in what we do in the near future. I'm just letting you know GOD has it, and GOD has us; so we won't have to worry about nothing. I appreciate everything you've done; not only for me, but also for my mom. That means the world to me, and from the bottom of my heart I love you dearly for that. There's nothing you could ever do to hurt me in any way, because what you did for my mom I could never imagine anyone else doing for her; so I appreciate that. What you've done for me you don't even know how I feel about it. You're outstanding as an uncle, but an even better human being whenever I needed someone to talk to. I've learned so much from you, and even though you might have thought I wasn't listening, I was. I took notes. I'm in the position I'm in today because I saw a young black man working and grinding hard, and now me and Frank Jr. are in that position; and it's all because of you. GOD blessed us with you, and I'm not going to take you for granted. I appreciate everything you've ever done for us. Whenever you need to retire then let us get this because we got it. You have three young adults over here ready to take it further than you've ever dreamed of. You wont' have to worry about anything, and my mom won't have to worry about anything because we got this."

Kevin Alexander Lee Jr.

Love Note: *to my brother*

"I'm proud of you and I'll always be there for you. I've always believed in you. Look at us now! Let's keep doing this. Let's keep looking forward, staying humble, and praising GOD. You're an awesome person. I'm pretty proud to say I'm your little sister. Love you."

Belinda Williams-Parker

Love Note: *to the family tree*

"Mother Carrie is beyond proud of all her children. She doesn't walk in bitterness, anger, or frustration. The origins of their family legacy are the consecutive result of her initiating her heist by moving north in the midst of the Civil Rights Movement. When she ran away, she didn't just run into her future she ran into her generational legacy...And doesn't even know it."

Mother Carrie's Legacy Heist

Quote before the Quest

"I once didn't want to share this story, not even with my kid's; because I thought the magnitude of the sacrifices I made would've been misunderstood. I could feel the depth of this story being written internally, but I knew I had to share this treasure with the world about twelve years ago. In the patience of not releasing this story, I saw that generational poverty was a pandemic in every society. This was my opportunity to deal with it; so I made the choice to eradicate the poverty inside myself, and add the authenticity of what my journey has been about since the beginning.

This is a choice that exist in every human being. The relevance of this story gives you access to redefine your own life-story, family members, legacy, and the narrative of what you mean to the world.

Wealth has been perceived as the haves and have-nots, but I've been beyond both sides. This generational curse is something I've seen with my own eyes in wealth, poverty, and everybody I originally thought had a polished lifestyle. This book brought me to tears, because it gave me an opportunity to set myself free. It was in a puddle of tears where I finally found peace, joy, and a pure connection to my own heart.

Until you read this book, you'll never have a conception of your own story in its entirety. It teaches you how to go back; and transfer generational legacy inside your family. Your true story is the relevance of your life; so take one chapter at a time, and note the things you want to address within the scope of your own life & family. Don't wait until generational poverty contaminates your wealth.... Initiate your legacy heist immediately, and forever redirect the paradigm of poverty in your family tree."

- Frank J. Williams

Printed in the USA
CPSIA information can be obtained
at www.ICGtesting.com
CBHW061607110324
5205CB00005B/12